DARTH VADER,
REBEL HUNTER!

Written by Lauren Nesworthy

Written by Lauren Nesworthy
Editor Tina Jindal
Art Editor Toby Truphet
Assistant Art Editors Ishita Chawla, Akansha Jain
DTP Designer Umesh Singh Rawat
Pre-production Producer Siu Yin Chan
Pre-production Manager Sunil Sharma
Senior Producer Alex Bell
Managing Editors Sadie Smith, Chitra Subramanyam
Managing Art Editors Neha Ahuja, Ron Stobbart
Publisher Julie Ferris
Art Director Lisa Lanzarini
Publishing Director Simon Beecroft

Reading Consultant Linda B. Gambrell

For Lucasfilm
Editorial Assistant Samantha Holland
Creative Director Michael Siglain
Image Archives Stacey Leong
Art Director Troy Alders
Story Group Leland Chee, Pablo Hidalgo, and Rayne Roberts

First American Edition, 2016
Published in the United States by DK Publishing
345 Hudson Street, New York, New York 10014

Page design copyright © 2016 Dorling Kindersley Limited
DK, a Division of Penguin Random House LLC
16 17 18 19 10 9 8 7 6 5 4 3 2 1
001–280783–July/2016

© & TM 2016 LUCASFILM LTD.

A catalog record for this book is
available from the Library of Congress.

ISBN: 978-1-4654-5213-9 (Hardback)
ISBN: 978-1-4654-5212-2 (Paperback)

DK books are available at special discounts when purchased in bulk
for sales promotions, premiums, fund-raising, or educational use. For details, contact:
DK Publishing Special Markets, 345 Hudson Street, New York, New York 10014
SpecialSales@dk.com

Printed and bound in China

A WORLD OF IDEAS:
SEE ALL THERE IS TO KNOW

www.dk.com
www.starwars.com

Contents

Who is Darth Vader?

Darth Vader is a Sith Lord. He is one of the most feared figures in the galaxy.

Vader shows no mercy. He will stop at nothing to destroy anyone who stands up to the Empire.

Vader has many loyal allies. They help him destroy enemies of the Empire.

MEET LORD VADER

He is dangerous, powerful, and always dressed in black armor. Darth Vader is not a man to cross. Even Imperial officers fear this mysterious Sith Lord who answers only to the Emperor.

Helmet protects the head

Goggles improve vision

Breathing device

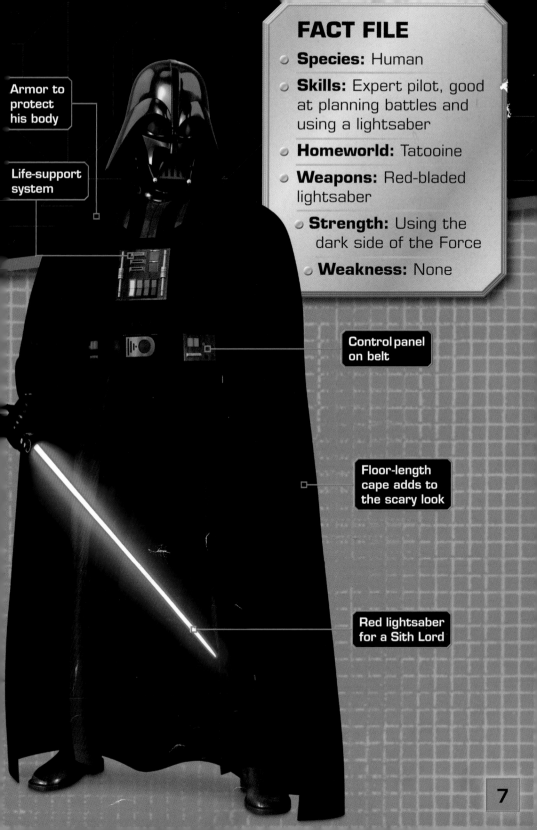

Armor to protect his body

Life-support system

FACT FILE

- **Species:** Human
- **Skills:** Expert pilot, good at planning battles and using a lightsaber
- **Homeworld:** Tatooine
- **Weapons:** Red-bladed lightsaber
- **Strength:** Using the dark side of the Force
- **Weakness:** None

Control panel on belt

Floor-length cape adds to the scary look

Red lightsaber for a Sith Lord

7

Fight for Freedom

A group of rebels are fighting back against the Empire.

More brave people are joining their fight. The Rebellion becomes harder to defeat.

The rebels have managed to escape every clever Imperial trap. Now Vader is determined to find a way to get rid of them—once and for all.

REBEL ALERT!

Beware, citizens of Lothal. A group of rebels has been creating trouble for the Empire. If you spot these criminals, tell an Imperial Officer straight away.

Name: Kanan Jarrus
Species: Human
Strength: Lightsaber and Jedi mind tricks
Weakness: Still learning to be a Jedi Knight

Wanted for being a Jedi

Name: Ezra Bridger
Species: Human
Strength: Is smart and has often tricked Imperial officers
Weakness: Mastering Jedi skills

Wanted for being a Padawan

Name: Ahsoka Tano
Species: Togruta
Strength: Strong Jedi abilities
Weakness: Tends to work alone

Wanted for plotting against the Empire

Name: Sabine Wren
Species: Human
Strength: Explosives expert
Weakness: Sometimes
too suspicious

Wanted for destroying Imperial property

Name: Hera Syndulla
Species: Twi'lek
Strength: Gifted pilot
Weakness: Tries to do
too much at once

Wanted for stealing shield generators

Name: Garazeb "Zeb" Orrelios
Species: Lasat
Strength: Expert at
close combat
Weakness: Losing his temper

Wanted for attacking Imperial Officers

Name: Chopper
Class: Astromech droid
Strength: Surprise electric shocks
Weakness: Sometimes
too stubborn

Wanted for acting like an Imperial droid

The Sith Lord

The rebels have no idea that Darth Vader was once a Jedi named Anakin Skywalker.

There was a time when he used the Force for good. However, he allowed anger and hate into his heart. He chose the dark side and became an evil Sith.

Darth Vader can use the dark side of the Force to control and defeat his enemies.

BEWARE
THE SITH

Sith are evil and use the dark side of the Force to destroy their enemies. Not much is known about the Sith. But one thing's for sure: there is nothing more scary than a powerful Sith Lord like Darth Vader.

The Sith use hate, fear, and greed to control the galaxy.

The Sith hate the Jedi who believe in peace.

The Sith can use lightning to destroy their enemies.

Only the most skilled Jedi can defeat a Sith Lord in a lightsaber battle.

There can only be two Sith Lords at one time.

The Sith will do anything for power.

Sith Rule of Two

There can only be two Sith at one time—a Master and an apprentice. This is called the Rule of Two.

The Emperor of the galaxy, Palpatine, is secretly the Sith Master! Darth Vader is his apprentice. He always obeys the Emperor's orders.

First Duel

Darth Vader is strong and powerful
in the ways of the dark side. He is
cunning and very skilled at fighting
with a lightsaber.

When rebels Kanan and Ezra
try to fight him, the Sith easily
defeats them. Kanan tells Ezra
that they were lucky to escape
with their lives!

JEDI vs SITH

It is almost impossible to defeat a Sith Lord. He is very good at using the lightsaber. But Kanan never backs down from a fight. He is a Jedi after all. So can he battle a Sith Lord?

Kanan Jarrus
Jedi Knight

Weapon: Blue lightsaber

Strength: Amazing fighting skills

Weakness: Has never fought a Sith Lord

Best Defense Tactic: To escape!

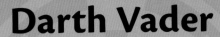

Darth Vader
Sith Lord

Weapon: Red lightsaber

Strength: Strong in the dark side of the Force

Weakness: None!

Best Offense Tactic: Using lies to make the rebels fear the Empire

Vader's Master Plan

An Imperial named Minister
Maketh Tua plans to help the rebels.
When Darth Vader discovers
her betrayal, he sets a trap for her.
He sees a chance to turn the people
of Lothal against the rebels!

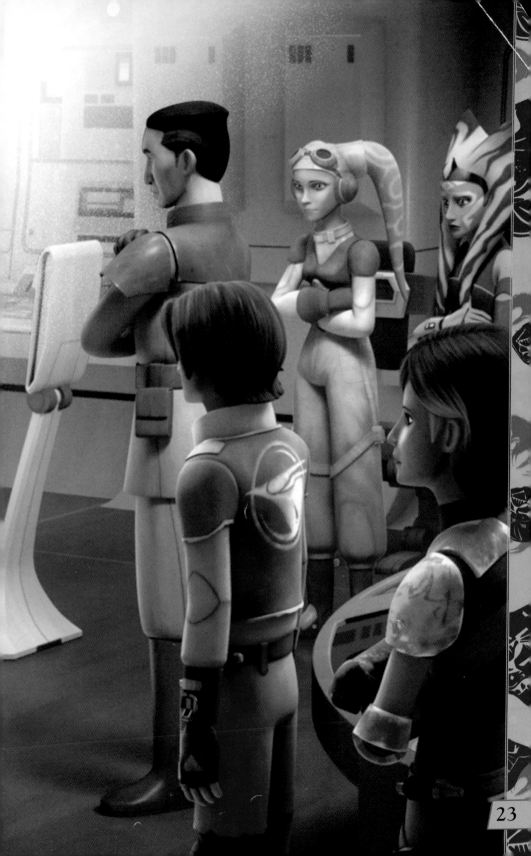

Traps and Tricks

When Minister Tua tries to run from
Lothal, she perishes in an explosion.
The Imperials tell everyone that
the rebels are to blame.

In fact, it was Darth Vader's
evil plan all along! His lies make
the rebels look like dangerous
criminals. Now they have to
leave Lothal.

Rebel Fleet Destroyed

The Rebel Alliance may be strong, but they do not have many ships.

Darth Vader follows the rebels to the small fleet, and he attacks it! The rebel base ship, Phoenix Home, is completely destroyed.

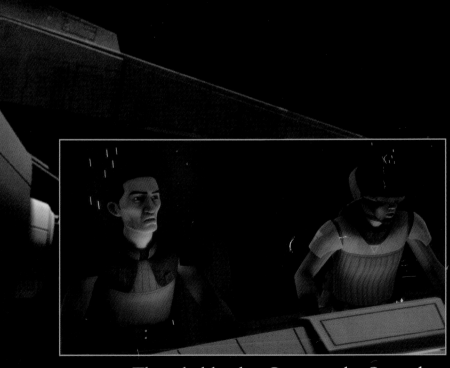

The rebel leader, Commander Sato, does not want to abandon Phoenix Home. But he has no choice. The ship is on fire!

Darth Vader has the perfect plan to catch
the rebels and destroy their base...

REBELS
WATCH OUT!

1

Set a trap for Minister Tua and the rebels. Place a bomb in an escape shuttle.

RESULT: The rebels escape but Minister Tua perishes.

2

Order Agent Kallus to send out a message on the radio, blaming the rebels for Minister Tua's death.

RESULT: The rebels are forced to hide.

Order the Imperials to burn Tarkintown. Arrest everyone living there, and draw the rebels out.

RESULT: The rebels have no choice but to escape Lothal.

Use the tracking device on the Imperial shuttle that the rebels stole. Follow them to their base.

RESULT: The rebel headquarters is discovered.

Attack the rebel fleet and capture the rebels alive.

RESULT: The rebels escape, but they are now much weaker!

A Secret Revealed

When Darth Vader attacks the rebel fleet, Ahsoka uses the Force to see how strong he is.

Ahsoka and Vader sense each
other through the Force. She is
shocked when she senses something
familiar about Vader.

Vader Hunts Ahsoka

Vader tells Emperor Palpatine
that Skywalker's apprentice
is still alive.

The evil Sith Lords believe that Ahsoka will lead them to other Jedi. They may even find powerful Jedi Master Obi-Wan Kenobi...

KNOW THE EMPIRE

Every official has a special role to play in the Empire.
Yet they all answer to the Emperor of
the galaxy... including Darth Vader.

SHEEV PALPATINE
Emperor

Sith Lord who rules
the galaxy.

WILHUFF TARKIN
Grand Moff

Makes sure that the
Empire is always powerful.

DARTH VADER
Sith Lord

Protects the Empire and
destroys all rebels.

KALLUS
ISB Agent

Hunts down rebels and
any remaining Jedi.

INQUISITORS
Jedi hunters

Hunt down hidden
Force-users—even children!

STORMTROOPERS
Imperial soldiers

Carry out the evil
orders of the Empire.

KASSIUS KONSTANTINE
Admiral

Commands the Star
Destroyer *Relentless*.

The Inquisitors

Inquisitors are specially trained
by the Empire to hunt Jedi.
Vader sends two Inquisitors,
Fifth Brother and Seventh Sister,
to capture the rebels.

The heroes may have defeated an Inquisitor before, but can they take on two?

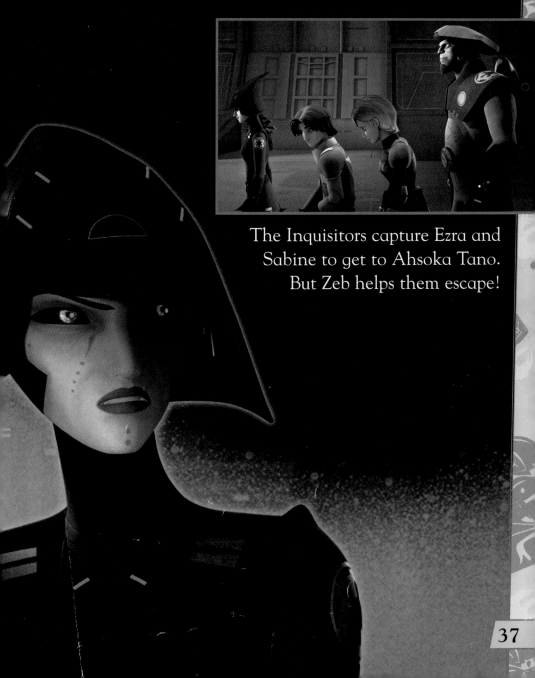

The Inquisitors capture Ezra and Sabine to get to Ahsoka Tano. But Zeb helps them escape!

The Fearless Jedi

Ahsoka must fight both Inquisitors
in a dangerous lightsaber battle.
The Inquisitors try to arrest her,
but they are no match for
her amazing Jedi skills!

Vader orders the Inquisitors to
capture Ahsoka. But she is too
quick for these Imperial Agents.

The Fight Goes On

The Empire is closing in on the Rebel Alliance.

The rebels are smart. They have managed to escape every Imperial trap so far.

However, they have no idea what Darth Vader is planning. They will soon face even greater danger.

The rebels will need all of their courage. The fight with Darth Vader is far from over.

Quiz

1. Who does Darth Vader always obey?

2. What is Darth Vader's weapon of choice?

3. Who is fighting back against the Empire?

4. Which side of the Force did Darth Vader choose?

5. Who do the Sith hate?

6. Which Imperial does Vader set a trap for?

7. Who do the Imperials blame for Minister Tua's death?

8. What is the name of the rebel base ship?

9. What was Darth Vader's name before he became a Sith?

10. Who did Vader send to capture the rebels?

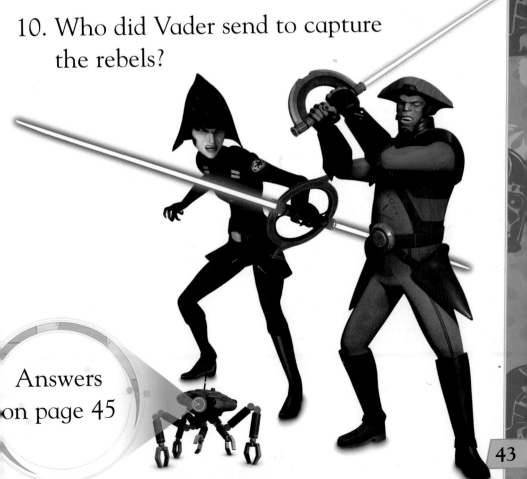

Answers on page 45

43

Glossary

Abandon
To leave behind with no plan of returning.

Allies
A group of people who work together for a purpose.

Apprentice
A person who works for someone else to
learn from them.

Betrayal
A break of trust by someone who you believed
was loyal to you.

Cunning
Very good at tricking people.

Dark Side
The evil side of the Force.

Empire
A group of nations ruled by one leader who is called an Emperor.

Expert
Someone who is very skilled at a particular thing.

Figure
An important person.

Force
The energy that flows through all living things.

Jedi Knight
A warrior with special powers who protects the galaxy from evil.

Lightsaber
A weapon used by Sith and Jedi warriors.

Padawan
A Jedi apprentice.

Perish
To be destroyed.

Rebel
Someone who fights against whoever is in power.

Tactic
A method of fighting during a battle.

Answers to the quiz on pages 42 and 43:
1. Emperor Palpatine 2. A red lightsaber 3. A group of rebels
4. The dark side 5. The Jedi 6. Minister Maketh Tua
7. The rebels 8. Phoenix Home 9. Anakin Skywalker
10. The Inquisitors

Guide for Parents

This book is part of an exciting four-level reading series for children, developing the habit of reading widely for both pleasure and information. These chapter books have a compelling main narrative to suit your child's reading ability. Each book is designed to develop your child's reading skills, fluency, grammar awareness, and comprehension in order to build confidence and engagement when reading.

Ready for a *Level 2* book

YOUR CHILD SHOULD

- be familiar with using beginning letter sounds and context clues to figure out unfamiliar words.
- be aware of the need for a slight pause at commas and a longer one at periods.
- alter his/her expression for questions and exclamations.

A VALUABLE AND SHARED READING EXPERIENCE

For many children, reading requires much effort, but adult participation can make this both fun and easier. So here are a few tips on how to use this book with your child.

TIP 1 Check out the contents together before your child begins:
- read the text about the book on the back cover.
- flip through the book and stop to chat about the contents page together to heighten your child's interest and expectation.
- make use of unfamiliar or difficult words on the page in a brief discussion.
- chat about the nonfiction reading features used in the book, such as headings, captions, lists, or charts.

TIP 2 Support your child as he/she reads the story pages:

- give the book to your child to read and turn the pages.

- where necessary, encourage your child to break a word into syllables, sound out each one, and then flow the syllables together. Ask him/her to reread the sentence to check the meaning.

- when there's a question mark or an exclamation mark, encourage your child to vary his/her voice as he/she reads the sentence. Demonstrate how to do this if it is helpful.

TIP 3 Chat at the end of each page:

- ask questions about the text and the meaning of the words used. These help to develop comprehension skills and awareness of the language used.

A FEW ADDITIONAL TIPS

- Always encourage your child to try reading difficult words by themselves. Praise any self-corrections, for example, "I like the way you sounded out that word and then changed the way you said it, to make sense."

- Try to read together everyday. Reading little and often is best. These books are divided into manageable chapters for one reading session. However, after 10 minutes, only keep going if your child wants to read on.

- Read other books of different types to your child just for enjoyment and information.

Series consultant **Dr. Linda Gambrell**, Distinguished Professor of Education at Clemson University, has served as President of the National Reading Conference, the College Reading Association, and the International Reading Association.

Index